"There is that old concept of the 'genius of a place,' which, as it enters literature, makes an atmosphere all its own—impossible to forget. I keep thinking of this as I read *My Hollywood and Other Poems*, in which Boris Dralyuk, the brilliant translator of Isaac Babel's *Odessa Stories*, now gives us Los Angeles: a theater of being, captured in beautifully crafted sonnets, pantoums, and hymns full of longing and character and verve. Anyone who has ever visited the Russian immigrant shops and restaurants of Los Angeles, or stopped in parks where old men play cards and grandmas watch kids while spreading gossip, will instantly recognize the music of memory in Dralyuk's virtuoso performance. The wit and daring of his rhymes and phrasing remind me of that old master, Donald Justice, who dazzled us with the elegance of his forms. Dralyuk carries this high style into the twenty-first century, and I, for one, am thrilled to be in the presence of his marvelous verbal art. Pay attention, readers: a new maestro is in our midst."

—**Ilya Kaminsky**, author of *Deaf Republic* and *Dancing in Odessa*

"Generations of Americans have chased their dreams to Los Angeles only to awake to strangeness and disappointment. In *My Hollywood* Boris Dralyuk brilliantly describes those dreamers' lives with the clear eye of an émigré who witnesses details that open up larger questions of life. Dralyuk is also a master of poetic craft whose meter and rhyme give his original work a classic flavor, and allow him to translate Russian poetry with skill, flare, and authenticity that is rare. *My Hollywood* is a book to savor."

—**A. M. Juster**, author of *Wonder & Wrath*

"*My Hollywood and Other Poems* works the shimmering depths and surfaces of a Russian presence in America's film-set. Its poems cross the refracted ache of exile with the kind of detail that narrates lives as precisely and suggestively as an Edward Hopper painting. A beautifully evocative debut."

—**Vona Groarke**, author of *Spindrift* and *Double Negative*

"Boris Dralyuk's *My Hollywood* is poignant and perfectly phrased, full of nostalgias and absences, home and exile, piercingly recognizable to anyone who loves the place and knows its failings. The inclusion of the other poets from the Russian diaspora provides a resonance of theme, but also highlights the unique charm of Dralyuk's verse."

—**Janet Fitch**, author of *White Oleander* and *Paint It Black*

"As a translator and anthologist, Boris Dralyuk has lovingly rescued neglected Russian poets, and he now achieves, in his own poems, a similar triumph with Los Angeles, recovering and preserving passages in its history that time and human indifference have obscured. *My Hollywood* features appearances by such cultural heavyweights as Thomas Mann, Laura and Aldous Huxley, and Arnold Schoenberg. But Dralyuk also treats us to tours of now vanished landmarks of L.A. like the Garden of Allah hotel and the Bargain Circus discount barn; and he chronicles the careers of some of the many entertaining misfits, including a ne'er-do-well uncle of Isaac Babel, who have passed through Southern California on their earthly pilgrimage. Dralyuk is as well a lively technician—a clever rhymer who is particularly deft at sonnets. Anyone interested in fine verse and Los Angeles will relish this book."

—**Timothy Steele**, author of *Toward the Winter Solstice*

MY HOLLYWOOD

AND OTHER POEMS

MY HOLLYWOOD

AND OTHER POEMS

BORIS DRALYUK

pdb

PAUL DRY BOOKS
Philadelphia 2022

First Paul Dry Books Edition, 2022

Paul Dry Books, Inc.
Philadelphia, Pennsylvania
www.pauldrybooks.com

Printed in the United States of America

Library of Congress Control Number: 2021951757

ISBN 978-1-58988-167-9

for my mother,
who brought me to Hollywood

CONTENTS

RUSSIAN HOLLYWOOD: TRANSLATIONS

LATE STYLE

ACKNOWLEDGMENTS

Versions of a number of these poems have appeared in journals, and I remain deeply grateful to the generous editors who responded so warmly to my submissions: Kathryn Gray and Andrew Neilson of *Bad Lilies*, Paula Deitz of *The Hudson Review*, David Garyan of *The International Literary Quarterly*, Ange Mlinko of *Subtropics*, Jackson Lears of *Raritan*, Jana Prikryl of *The New York Review of Books*, David Yezzi of *The Hopkins Review*, Gerald Maa of *The Georgia Review*, A.M. Juster of *First Things*, Quincy R. Lehr of *The Raintown Review*, Melissa Balmain of *Light*, Adam Kirsch of *The New Criterion*, J.D. McClatchy of *The Yale Review*, and Richard Berengarten of *Jewish Quarterly*. I am just as grateful to André de Korvin, Edouard Boghossian, and Wladislaw Ellis for permission to translate the work of their fathers, Vladimir Korvin-Piotrovsky, Richard Ter-Boghossian, and Vladislav Ellis, and to Kay Duke Ingalls for permission to translate the work of Vernon Duke. I have made every effort to locate living relatives of Peter Vegin, but, unfortunately, none have been found. Five marvelous Angelenos have been a constant source of support and inspiration over the years, drawing many of these poems directly out of me: Dana Gioia, Roman Koropeckyj, Oscar Mandel, Lisa Teasley, and Stephen Yenser. And three friends and teachers from other points on the globe have filled each of my days with the music of their work: Maria Bloshteyn, Robert Chandler, and Irina Mashinski. I have had the great fortune to meet, at the Crossroads of the World, colleagues who have become like family to me; they all have my gratitude, and I offer special thanks to Tom Lutz for welcoming me into the fold in 2011. Paul Dry, Julia Sippel, and Mara Brandsdorfer of Paul Dry Books are an author's dream of a publishing team. Most importantly, without the love, encouragement, and enlivening suggestions of my wife and partner in all things, Jenny Croft, I would never have thought this book worth making.

MY HOLLYWOOD

for Dana Gioia,
the bard of Chandler country

MY HOLLYWOOD: A TRIPTYCH

I. Aspiration

> That night I discovered the park at De Longpre and
> Cherokee. . . . Looking at all the small houses, telling myself
> that these were where Swanson and Pickford and Chaplin
> and Arbuckle and the others used to live in the good
> old days . . .
>
> —Horace McCoy, 1938

This much is clear: the good old days have passed.
Some giant fig trees, a few pygmy palms
drop broken shade on disenfranchised grass;
dogs loping, limping; vagrants begging alms;
and in the center—ludicrously named
Aspiration—face uplifted, framed
by dusty fronds, he stands on tippy-toe,
abstract Adonis, bronze lothario.
Sit here all night, if you can bear the grime—
watch people come and go, but you will see no
women in black shed tears for Valentino.
The Sheik sinks deep into the dunes of time.
A crow clacks in the branches overhead,
like a projector slowly going dead.

II. The Flower Painter

> The château was also demolished, but don't go thinking
> this was an imaginary château. Inquiries made, it was the
> residence of Monsieur Paul de Longpré, a French painter who
> had lived here since the beginning of Hollywood . . .
>
> —Blaise Cendrars, 1936

A scruffy rose bush puts on airs out front
a big beige box—two stories, caked in stucco—
that bears the name, in flaking cursive font,
of Paul de Longpré. Fainter than an echo,
the long-departed flower painter's ghost
patrols the grounds, where he for years played host
to pleasure-seekers in his man-made Eden.
Decades ago, that Eden went to seed and
it pains me to recall what is no more . . .
My Hollywood, *mon vieux*, is not ideal:
a grand old dame reduced to dishabille,
her glory far too faded to restore.
But ruin was inscribed in what he built.
His precious blossoms? They were sure to wilt.

Boris Dralyuk

III. The Garden of Allah

> The Garden of Allah Hotel, playground of the movie stars
> during the 20s and 30s, will be torn down to make way for a
> new commercial and business center. . . . The hotel originally
> was the home of Alla Nazimova, late stage and screen star.
>
> —*Los Angeles Mirror-News*, 1959

And now I watch another era fade,
Cyrillic letters scraped from shuttered storefronts,
tar-crusted bread, stale fish, stiff marmalade
sit sulking on the shelves, unchosen orphans
in what were once the bustling little shops
of Russian Hollywood. Hardly a soul now stops
to thumb the plums, frown at the penciled prices;
the neighborhood is lurching towards crisis,
all in slow motion. Rents climb out of reach
for émigrés . . . There's nothing new in this.
Think of Nazimova and of her short-lived bliss
beside her pool—her private Black Sea beach . . .
She died a tenant in a bungalow
of a hotel razed sixty years ago.

UNIVERSAL HORROR

> Hollywood Movie Posters is the oldest memorabilia store
> in the world located in the same location with the same
> proprietor. . . . You can find the shop tucked away in
> Artisan's Patio, an alleyway off of Hollywood Blvd.
>
> —KABC, March 19, 2020

All through the first great war to end all wars,
the siren-addled nights of its successor,
up till last week, the sunbaked, time-warped doors
of one slim passage welcomed every passer-
by . . . High noon, yet no one passes by . . .
Magnetic trinkets draw no tourist's eye.
Motes build tract housing in the grooves of vinyl.
An eerie calm prevails. Not tomblike—shrinal.
I come for solace. Far in back, vitrines
hold Universal Monsters safely penned:
vampires, mummies, wolf men—every friend
of anxious childhood, surest of vaccines
against the grownup world's uncertain horrors,
which spread like scentless, soundless fog before us.

Boris Dralyuk

THE PASSING OF THE BUNGALOWS

The bungalow courts extended at least a touch of 'casual
California living' even to the poor.
　　　　　　　—Robert Winter, *The California Bungalow* (1980)

They held their courts from here to Pasadena,
not in regalia but in plainer clothes,
withholding judgment on our misdemeanors,
warm, down-to-earth, arrayed in close-knit rows—
no hint of hauteur to these Swiss chalets,
these beaming Tudors, Spanish hideaways
that dignified us with lagniappes of style:
crown moulding, copper awning, clinker tile.
Fair bungalows, now your dominion comes
to closure. I watch swaths of you demolished
in favor of the featureless and polished
plutocracy of condominiums.
Your bold agaves, fierce, protective aloes
lay down their spears beside the realtors' gallows.

CLOSE TO HOME

> The dingbat typifies Los Angeles apartment building
> architecture at its worst.
>
> —Leonard and Dale Pitt, *Los Angeles A to Z* (1997)

Some years ago I learned they call them "dingbats,"
these proud but shambly veterans at rest,
who lean on carport columns as on muskets,
one tarnished decoration on each chest—
a rust-red star or an abraded crest.

An ugly name. It makes me feel indignant
on their behalf: Haven't they done their best
to serve with honor? Can they not be trusted
to guard the tempest-tossed, the dispossessed,
the migratory species of the West?

Their rooms, unfurnished, furnish everything that
we birds of paradise require for a nest.
So what if half the cabinets are busted,
the front door warped, the carpeting distressed?
Fly free. They will not hold you. You're their guest.

THE BUREAU OF STREET LIGHTING

> A Bureau of Street Lighting was created within the
> Department of Public Works in 1925, which establishes
> criteria for all street lighting and determines locations of the
> lighting units.
>
> —Eddy S. Feldman, *The Art of
> Street Lighting in Los Angeles* (1972)

What would we be without the light you lend us?
Hard to imagine what we were back when . . .
A desert pueblo, sleepy haciendas
with smoke-stained lanterns blinking out by ten.

Yes, I suppose I'll thank you for the darkness
your light supports: the luring night-bound streets,
the anonymity of motels and apartments,
all the small trade that's done without receipts.

Yes, for the city limit, for your tactless,
incessant focus on just who we are.
You will not let the zodiac distract us—
you make our private misery the star.

BARGAIN CIRCUS

So it goes at Bargain Circus, perhaps L.A.'s most whimsical discount store. . . . The eclectic selection of goods and guilt-inducing low prices draw a melange of Orthodox Jews, Russians, Armenians and Westside connoisseurs.

—*Los Angeles Times*, 1997

Clown prince of bargain shops—those penny-ante
Xanadus that take up half a block—
was the La Brea Circus. Huge barn chock-
full of overstock, a poor man's horn of plenty,

where we, though broke as sparrows, like canaries
flitted about, whistled with disbelief
at deals—no, steals!—that would abash a thief:
Bic pens for nickels, dollar dictionaries!

I wore my Webster's out, clumsily wooing
the tongue in which I sing this dime store's praise.
But they're worn too, my memories of those days,
like VHS tapes after years of viewing

and spooling backwards to the sweetest spot.
Oh yes, that was another thing we bought:
a plastic sports-car VHS rewinder—
so obsolete, so perfectly designed for

its vanished purpose, like a streamlined hearse
inexorably heading in reverse.

Boris Dralyuk

ÉMIGRÉ LIBRARY

Our library is open, but for whom?
The ranks of the expired far outnumber
these half-blind holdouts hobbling through the room.

Surely our yellowed labels all spell doom
in letters too few learn, too few remember.
Our library is open, but for whom?

They don't disturb our poets' mildewed gloom
or rouse our Realists from their dreamless slumber,
these half-blind holdouts hobbling through the room.

What do we hope for? Someone to exhume
a priceless birchbark from our heaps of lumber?
Our library is open, but for whom?

We know their scent (that deafening perfume)
and preference (always romance, nothing somber),
these half-blind holdouts hobbling through the room—

just as we know the posture they assume
when they first enter: straight-backed, unencumbered.
Our library is open, but for whom?
These half-blind holdouts hobbling through the room.

PANTOUM OF PLUMMER PARK

Felled patriarchs, deracinated, lame,
they plant themselves at parks on folding chairs
for Préférence—a hoary plain-trick game—
to pass the time, to whist and bid misère.

They plant themselves at parks on folding chairs,
who once could not have spared a daylit hour,
and pass the time, and whist or bid misère,
like spellbound warriors robbed of their power.

Who once could not have spared a daylit hour
now look intently at their idle hands
like spellbound warriors robbed of their power,
feeling the futile draw of distant lands.

Now look intently at their idle hands:
those muted throbs, those twitches they restrain
tell of the futile draw of distant lands,
of what they were, of what they must remain—

felled patriarchs, deracinated, lame.

Boris Dralyuk

THE MINOR MASTERS

On Santa Monica I know someone who'll etch
forms of a hair's breadth in a rubber stamp.
No molds or lasers: just the human touch.
If darkness overwhelms an heirloom lamp,

head west on Beverly, and east of Kings you'll find
Pairpoint's prometheus. If age brittles a book,
on Cahuenga there's a man who'll bind
its outcast leaves. Such people make things look

immune to time and innocent of pain,
intact, immaculate, as none of us remain.
Long live the masters whose quaint crafts are holy.
They work in solitude. Now by appointment only.

STRAVINSKY AT THE FARMERS MARKET

The bloom worn off Vedanta's lotus,
the war looming, Maria and Aldous Huxley
take Katia and Thomas Mann
for a stroll along the breakers.

"At our feet," recalled Huxley, "the sand
was covered with small whitish objects,
like dead caterpillars. Recognition dawned."
"Many condoms on the beach," wrote Mann.

Christopher Isherwood is a disciple, slipping
off to the Viertels on the weekends: far from Swami,
swimming naked. In Brentwood, Schoenberg lobs grapefruits
and insults at Feuchtwanger's wife.

Herr Doktor Faustus, exile is no bargain.
You move *von heute auf morgen.*
Stravinsky lunches at the Farmers Market.
The Firebird is plucked, Petrushka's henpecked.

The new addresses, the unlisted numbers.
All smiles and miniature flags, your exile meets you
        at the airport,
shows you around a little—the Egyptian, Forest Lawn—
then drops you off at the Marmont.

Boris Dralyuk

BABEL AT THE KIBITZ

> My uncle Lev, my father's brother, had studied at the Yeshiva
> in Volozhin. In 1892 he escaped conscription and abducted
> the daughter of a quartermaster serving in the Kiev military
> district. Uncle Lev took this woman to California, to Los
> Angeles, abandoned her there, and died in a madhouse
> among Negroes and Malays. After his death, the American
> police sent us our inheritance from Los Angeles—a big
> trunk bound with brown iron hoops. This trunk held
> dumbbells, locks of women's hair, Uncle's tallith, whips with
> gilded handles, and herbal tea in little boxes trimmed with
> cheap pearls.
>
> —Isaac Babel, "The Story of My Dovecot"

I see you now, a scrawny Levantine
swilling the rotgut on the Calle de los Negros
shoulder to shoulder with the Chinese and Malays—
the great black sheep of the Odessa Babels.

Lassoed by day-dreams, sped along by whips
with gilded handles, tall tales from Mayne Reid,
you quit the Pale and lit out for the States
with all the chutzpah of a one-eyed drayman.

Shaking the Keystone Kops of Kiev—that was rich.
But the poor shiksa, how you left her twisting
in her first Santa Anas—not a stitch
of decent clothes, and not a word of English . . .

And there you were, with whores and panel-thieves,
the sundry chiselers of every crumbling seaside.
You find what you were after, Uncle Lev?
You ditched Odessa for a new Odessa.

A syphilitic luftmensch run to ground,
weighed down by dumbbells in a Boyle Heights madhouse,
forever stuck between two sweetly rotten towns.
I hope you're proud. I hope you're shepping naches

over your nephew, who did good with your big trunk.
But let's not kvetch. Let's go and hit the Kibitz.
We've got no urgent business. Let's get drunk
where ACs burr and wheeze like old hasidim.

The LA sky's a quinceañera by Chagall.
Schlemiels like us—we never quit the Pale.

Boris Dralyuk

ABSENTEE BALLET

ABSENTEE BALLET

Today I cast my absentee ballet.
*Re*cast, I mean. It's in its umpteenth season.
I've added parts. I add parts every day.
The house lights dim and the new dancers breeze in—
so like the wispy, skeletal remains
of fallen leaves, those bare and brittle veins.
They take position, pirouette, jeté.
How could I turn a single one away?
And so it grows: a cast of thousands now.
The stage boards creak beneath tiptoeing figures
of memory. I whistle to the riggers:
the curtain drops. Time for a final bow.
Each day I scour the papers for reviews,
but find obituaries, crosswords, and old news.

CALENDARS

Surely, I must turn a new leaf.
I am a new leaf turning . . .
   —Henri Coulette

One to a cell, some thirty to a block,
they spend long hours staring at the clock,

while all their constant motions and appeals
go nowhere, nowhere, and their three square meals

are left untouched. There's simply no relief
for these dead-enders at the Château d'If.

And so they do their time, their months of yearning.
Turn a new leaf . . . A new leaf turning . . .

PLANTS IN POTS

for Samuel Menashe

Calm captives, inch by inch, they make their flight,
and reach the window, bent on seeing light.

THE DRINK

I raise the water up
to meet the tub's chipped lip.
I am what I displace—
the runoff from the dip,
clear as the thing I waste.
I am my albatross;
wearing myself, I hope
to make up for my loss.

NOTATION

In certain rooms I lived
  like momentary noise.
In others, I took pains
  to make myself perceived.
In some I was the creak
  to be more felt than heard—
  linoleum's absurd
  and personal mystique.
In many I was shrill—
  the pealing song of birds
  accustomed to the scraps
  left on the windowsill.
In yours I wasn't sound,
  I was the tangled sheet
  still clinging to your feet,
  holding your ankles bound.

TRANS-ATLANTIC

Journeying home—the wrong side of the road,
a world away. I am a bead of blood
that struggles up an artery, against the tide,
to find the heart that I have left behind.

Boris Dralyuk

OLD FLAME

Above the tongue-tip is an air so blue
I can compare it only to how you,
who once consumed me in a yellow heat,
now scarcely singe me when we meet.

JONAH

Was this the end? He couldn't rightly say.
There was no light. He lost all track of time.
If there was rumbling, it was too sublimely
steady to discern. Senses betrayed him.

Except, of course, there was the mealy smell
of his unlucky neighbors. Scales and slime
stuck to his fingers, too. He thought the climate
was hellish, even for a fish's belly.

It's true, at first he did give in to tears,
but these soon mingled with the brine and dried.
And in the end he grew to like the calm.

He hadn't written anything in years,
but something in the rhythm of the tide . . .
He offered up a little psalm.

Boris Dralyuk

THE CATCH: ON TRANSLATION

I draw you out, faint voice, from rippled pages:
a famished angler reeling in a fish,
the kind that, in the folktale, grants a wish—
a golden thing, imbued with living magic.

Between us is the taut line of attention,
imperiled by the current and the wind.
Slowly but willfully, I reel you in.
We hold each other, for a moment, in suspension.

RUSSIAN TREFOIL

I. For Innokenty Annensky (1855–1909)

You prefer wordless songs, children's cries
to a silence too easily filled
with black thoughts—unbidden, unwilled.
You would settle for shimmering lies,

yet they wither more quickly than roses.
Lamenting how badly they age,
you entrust your despair to the page
as another day closes.

II. For Georgy Ivanov (1894–1958)

Take a small table on the sidewalk,
the one that's farthest from the door,
in such a way that no one wonders
if you were here the day before.

It is as if you've signed a contract
to sit here like a statuette.
How well you know the terms that bind you:
boredom, and pity, and neglect.

III. For Yevgeny Kropivnitsky (1893–1979)

If the earth were smaller,
if it were no bigger
than a purblind suburb,
if it were a meager
row of wooden barracks,
and if time should curl
like a cat's sleek tail
round this curtal world—
you would be my neighbor,
I would come right over,
we'd forget our labors,
sit around the stove or
maybe go out strolling,
while the universe
proceeded on its course—
cooling, cooling, cooling . . .

Boris Dralyuk

RUSSIAN HOLLYWOOD:
TRANSLATIONS

for Robert Chandler,
a master of the art

Vladimir Korvin-Piotrovsky
1891–1966

EXILE'S RETURN

To perform a final honor,
a sleek cruiser from Kronstadt
sails into the silent harbor
slowly, like a juggernaut.
Ready for its distant journey,
taking leave of foreign lands,
comes a light-weight coffin, swaying
through a sea of lowered heads.
Were we right or wrong? No matter:
flag's at half-mast on the stern.
With its scrap of Russian glory
in the hold, the vessel turns.
Such great heights, such depths below . . .
Joyful foam sprays everywhere
and a farewell siren bellows,
lonely, in the azure air.
All those stars and all those countries—
the return he had long sought . . .
A thick northern fog engorges
the thin-throated Kattegat.
As it nears the Gulf of Finland
through the Baltic—drizzly, dull—
waves, serene yet unrelenting,
beat against the cruiser's hull.
In the brief glare from the lighthouse,

they rise up and pass away:
clouds and islands, clouds and islands,
blots of smoke, a barren quay.

1961

Vladimir Korvin-Piotrovsky

"WE'RE GOING FISHING"

We're going fishing. Early morning.
The overheated engine whines.
Quivering layers of desert air
float off toward the hills beyond.
A sandy wasteland—lifeless, bare—
but it's a joy to watch the sky.
Where fearless Native chiefs once roamed,
death strikes no fear. Let arrows fly.
An eagle's heart lies in the dunes,
mourned by the desiccated steppe.
Our driver points: a chain of trees,
all green, already looms ahead.
Ridge after ridge. The Colorado
lures with its unseen depths of blue . . .
O Russia—you're so far away now
that I can never part with you.

June 1, 1961, Los Angeles

Vernon Duke (Vladimir Dukelsky)
1903–1969

FARMERS MARKET

Plump little clouds, like rolls of bread,
lie on the sky's blue tablecloth.
The sun is orange marmalade
scooped generously from the jar.
Breakfast is ready, it would seem,
but we will never reach that high—
besides, our time has not yet come:
we're plenty happy where we are.
Just show us to the Farmers Market,
that citadel of gluttony,
lavish abode fit for Lucullus,
where fruits and vegetables and flowers
arch like a rainbow over earth
and dazzle countless looky-loos.
The meat upon a nearby tray
is ruddy with ferocious health—
at any moment it might leap
right down and turn into a calf.
A fresh-caught fish puffs out its cheeks
and gives a crab a flirty wink;
its scales still drip with salty water,
all iridescent, nacre-like.
Bronze-colored coffee from Brazil
does battle with the sea's strong smell,
but both are in the end defeated

Boris Dralyuk

by the aroma of the dill,
the savory odor of Dutch cheese,
the serenade of gorgonzola.
To right and left are restaurants,
and also strangers, apparitions—
but not the type you find in Blok,
just average girls, everyday women.
Beautiful Ladies don't abound.
Some are in trousers, some in skirts.
No mysteries—it's clear as day:
teeth gleaming, bosoms ample, fragrant—
all attributes are on display,
and there's no need to get acquainted.
Let's sit down at the nearest table,
and I will go and fetch—your choice!—
Mexican rice flavored with saffron,
a salmon of the palest pink,
a lobster with two piercing whiskers,
sweet buttered cobs of golden corn . . .
Perhaps Italian minestrone?
Or a gray soup of swallow's nests,
prepared, of course, a la Chinoise?
There is no perfume, no thick fog—
all is so obvious, so plain,
and tuneful without any music:
a purely thoughtless tenderness,
uncomplicated happiness—
and that, my dear, will do for us.

January 1, 1962

Vernon Duke

SUNSET STRIP

Poor lady is in tatters,
disheveled and distressed—
a star of yesterday.

Abandoned by the cameras,
no wonder she's depressed:
her heart is drained away.

Look all you like, no matter—
won't guess how old she is . . .
Her dress is dull and gray:

despite her stately manners,
she can't keep up appearances
without her former pay.

Her days drag on, relentless,
her eyes look tired and lifeless,
her furs are worn and frayed . . .

O Hollywood, how horrid . . .
Lord, work your little wonders:
restore her faded fame.

Boris Dralyuk

Richard Ter-Boghossian
1911–2005

HOLLYWOOD

Your air, Los Angeles, is poisoned
with the exhaust of countless cars.
You're famous—yes, the whole world knows you,
knows all your grand and minor stars.

Gangsters of every form and fashion
drift through your bars, your parks, your streets.
O verdant town of sinful passions,
forever drenched in sunlight, heat.

Lush greenery hides handsome villas—
I loved them at first sight, still do.
True, subterranean forces quiver—
man can endure a fright or two.

City of Angels . . . Standing guard
are rows of palms, stately and thin.
But we—we trample on our dusty stars,
and that is Hollywood's great sin.

Vladislav Ellis
1913–1975

CALIFORNIAN VERSES

1.

So as to squeeze the sweetest juice
(why pour a drink no one can stand?),
throughout these verses I will use
oranges, women, sun and sand.

Give in, relax, give up your past,
and it will make you young again:
the Californian beach—so vast,
for every class and shade of skin.

There's space enough for everyone!
Oranges, women—can't be beat.
Of course, the pastries of Ukraine
would make the pleasure feel complete.

2.

Don't fret about the heat too much:
evening will bring its cooling touch.

Our climate diligently clears
the heart of all its aches and fears.

Stepping outside to get some air,
a gentle breeze brushing their hair

Boris Dralyuk

beneath the Californian sky,
little old ladies grow more spry.

3.

A Scandinavian essence rings
within the sound of Spanish names:
that's why I love, I must confess,
this flashy, multicolored mess.

There's plenty room for all one's thoughts,
which whirl about and glow and flare.
Armenians find Ararat
while Finns find birches everywhere.

So you've been wronged by destiny,
your love is in some far-off land—
however hard your luck may be,
you'll always find a countryman.

Vladislav Ellis

A MEXICAN BIRCH

We disfigure nature
to disrupt life's flatness.
I plant a little birch tree
beside a prickly cactus,

and instantly regret it . . .
How I mourn for her—
an orphan in the desert,
a spindly foreigner.

She'll dwell here, never hearing
spring's lighthearted song.
Heat slayed her catkin-earring:
barely burst—now gone.

Fearfully, her slender
trunk bends with the wind.
All migrants understand her:
it's hard without a friend.

Boris Dralyuk

Peter Vegin (1939–2007)

"ARMENIANS UNHURRIEDLY"

Armenians unhurriedly
walk through the streets of Hollywood,
bearing lavash, khinkali, greens,
all that they'd grown accustomed to
where Ararat blocks half the sky,
where Ararat fills up your soul
so that you never can escape,
even halfway around the world.

True love for women or for mountains
is all the same—a sacred poison—
no matter what, there's no deliverance.
Go on, then: live, try to remember,
and if your memory should fail you,
your loved one will still find you, always.

This morning I awoke in Hollywood
to springtime, hummingbirds, magnolias,
and from my balcony I spotted
my dear Armenians, unhurried . . .
While in the sky above—what's that?
The great, the holy Ararat . . .

LATE STYLE

LATE STYLE

But late evening, late blossoms, and late autumns
are perfectly punctual.

—Michael Wood

For ages I've awaited my late style.
The bread grew stale. The candles shrank and guttered.
Busboys refilled my glass. After a while
the waiter took the menu, softly muttered,
"Poor sap," and left a bill for the chianti.
And still I sit, tapping my fingers, wanting
to see it, hear it—wide-eyed, short of breath,
begging forgiveness, drenched and pale as death.
I wonder what excuses it'll make:
work, weather, traffic? Doesn't really matter.
Well worth the wait. I listen to the chatter
at other tables—youthful, easy, fake.
I'll keep my vigil till I turn to stone,
stubbornly silent, artlessly alone.

UNCREDITED

No breakout leads—a prisoner of reruns
on local stations high up on the dial:
a stray recurring role, a guest appearance
on *Perry Mason*. Later, *Rockford Files*.

Her second act? Pure dullsville in Van Nuys.
Chablis with ice. A Chevy dealership
gone belly up. Her paunchy husband's lies:
a broken marriage. Then a broken hip.

None of that matters, if you ever catch her
singing "How High the Moon"—silvery, misty—
on that one show . . . She isn't any match for
the stainless Julie London or June Christy,

but through her gauzy voice, as through a sieve,
spare notes of heaven reach you from afar.
For those two minutes, she'll make you believe:
Somewhere there's music. It's where you are.

Boris Dralyuk

R. B. KITAJ'S "LOS ANGELES"

Impossible to say he was diminished,
or that his final efforts were unfinished.

Each fallow plane of color, each bald spot
of canvas was the harvest of long thought.

The early work, on which his learning lay
in patches of midrashic appliqué,

broke down to this one solomonic plea,
myrrh-scented murmur: *Lover, come to me.*

And she, at the expense of earthly things,
returned, perfected, on angelic wings.

VENICE BEACH: A DIPTYCH

I. Sarah Bernhardt, 1913

> Uncertain now, with faltering steps, but indomitable, she
> played half-hour performances in vaudeville programs . . .
> —Lois Foster Rodecape, 1941

Fatigued, divine, she steps out on the boards
of Kinney Pier. The dark Pacific water
waves its white kerchief: foam, at least, accords
due adulation . . . Not the train that brought her:
it rattled rudely. And this funny town—
a new-world Venice—looks a bit rundown.
When she turns back, her hotel's drab façade
sends a cold greeting from the esplanade.
Quand même, tonight, in what they call *"Camille,"*
she'll die her death and prove herself immortal.
Age cannot blunt her power to transport all
these crowds who come expecting vaudeville.
The sun has set. She must not miss her cue
to bid Los Angeles her last adieu.

Boris Dralyuk

II. Alexander Drankov, 1930

> An obscure retoucher in a photographer's shop in one of the
> cities in the Jewish Pale of Settlement . . . he became the first,
> and for a long time, the only film producer in Russia.
>
> —Lou Reech, 1923

> Drankov tried many things—went from high Hollywood
> hopes to a boardwalk cafe in Venice, California . . . when
> I last saw him he operated a small photo-finishing plant in
> San Francisco.
>
> —Jay Leyda, 1960

Oil derricks lower like Petliura's troops
at Kinney Pier: in Venice, crude is king.
Aboard the Volga Boat, fake Cossacks whoop
in frenzied indigence, real colonels bring
out rafts of breaded chicken and skewered mutton,
enough to stuff the gut of any glutton,
had any gluttons showed . . . The night's a flop.
Tomorrow he'll start over, from the top,
or from the bottom. In Constantinople
he raced cockroaches, in Yalta he shot porn.
(So what? Was "Goldwyn" to the studio born?)
As buoyant as a cork, constantly hopeful,
Drankov sails on, until he lands, at last,
in the vinegary darkrooms of his past.

BALLADE OF HANK'S BAR

> The narrow bar—a few booths and 14 stools—is attached to
> the 80-year-old Stillwell Hotel.
>
> —*Los Angeles Times*, 1997

Remember the wobbly barstool? The pleather
as red as the sore on what's-her-name's lip?
And how she would curl that lip whenever
you'd slide her a couple of coins for a tip?
Where is the tumbler of bourbon you'd sip?
Where's its amigo, the Mexican beer—
Pacifico, wasn't it? Down with the ship . . .
Sunk are the dives of yesteryear.

Where are the Stillwell's transient residents?
The gap-toothed cook, ready to brawl?
The queenly lush? We'd watch her hesitant
steps through the lobby, afraid she'd fall
and just as afraid she'd outlive us all . . .
Who'll nurse her sherry, turn a deaf ear
to bangs and whimpers, even last call?
Sunk are the dives of yesteryear.

Where are their faces of silly putty?
Their exhalations of acetone?
And where are you, my boozy buddy—
hanged or banished, like poor Villon?
Too far gone to pick up the phone?
I always knew you would disappear,

leave me to settle the tab alone . . .
Sunk are the dives of yesteryear.

Somewhere, somewhere the bars are open
and cheap as dirt, or so I hear . . .
You feeling no pain? Here's hoping . . .
But sunk are the dives of yesteryear.

DICTIONARY OF OMISSIONS

> The chief shortcoming of the *Dictionary* is, paradoxically,
> that it is so good that one wishes it were larger . . .
> —*Modern Language Review*

The atlas of my sunken continents,
the empty bowl I used to keep my fish in,
the shoebox of expired pawn tickets,
and this—my *Dictionary of Omissions*.
Words I'd withheld like an obsessive hoarder
have been arrayed in alphabetic order
by some unsparing lexicographer.
Forever at a loss, I now refer
to brave objections that I should have made,
to simple kindnesses never extended,
conclusions left obscenely open-ended,
heart-rending breaks faint-heartedly delayed.
The supplements arrive, set after set—
perpetual addenda of regret.

LETHE

Nothing was ever
quite the same.

Every one came
to be another.

This is a river
that goes by the name

of the river I
will never recover.

Boris Dralyuk is the Editor in Chief of the *Los Angeles Review of Books*. His poems have appeared or are forthcoming in *The New York Review of Books, The Hopkins Review, The New Criterion, The Yale Review, First Things, Subtropics, The Georgia Review*, and elsewhere. He is co-editor (with Robert Chandler and Irina Mashinski) of *The Penguin Book of Russian Poetry*, editor of *1917: Stories and Poems from the Russian Revolution* and *Ten Poems from Russia*, and translator of Isaac Babel, Mikhail Zoshchenko, and other authors. Dralyuk holds a Ph.D. in Slavic Languages and Literatures from UCLA, and has taught there and at the University of St Andrews. He lives in Los Angeles.